FATTY LIVE FRYER COOKBOOK FOR BEGINNERS

1500 DAYS OF QUICK AND HEALTHY RECIPES TO REVERSE FATTY LIVER AND CLEANSE YOUR BODY

HELEN TAYLOR

Introduction

A gourmand at heart, Helen had always been. She had always been a voracious eater since she was a little child. She particularly like fried food, particularly chicken wings and french fries. Although she became older, she never lost her love of eating, although she did gain weight.

Helen noticed that her energy levels were declining while she was in her mid-thirties. Because of her constant fatigue, getting out of bed in the mornings was getting more and more difficult. She was gaining weight as well, and her clothing was becoming increasingly tight.

According to her doctor, she had a fatty liver, which was most likely brought on by her love of fried foods. Helen felt both dismay and disbelief. If she desired to live a long, healthy life, she understood that she had to change.

It was more difficult than Helen anticipated for her to stop eating fried foods, but she tried. She regretted having missed the flavour and crispiness. She attempted baking several of her favourites, but they just didn't turn out right. She came upon the air fryer at that time.

All of Helen's favourite fried dishes could now be enjoyed guilt-free thanks to the air fryer. Though she was doing it in a healthy way, she might still give in to her urges. She had more energy and started to slim down. Even her general health seemed to have improved.

In her air fryer, Helen started experimenting with various recipes, and the results astounded her. Everything from chicken wings to onion rings could be made by her and turned out just as crispy and delectable as the fried counterparts.

There are a lot of other individuals out there who are dealing with the same problems that Helen had to deal with, she realised as she investigated the realm of air frying more. She was aware that people who were trying to better their own lives needed to hear about her knowledge and experience.

This is how the "Fatty Liver Air Fryer Cookbook for Beginners" came to be. Helen put in many hours to develop a collection of dishes that were not only scrumptious but also healthful. She wished to demonstrate to others that it was possible to partake in one's favourite dishes without losing either flavour or wellbeing.

Inspiring others to take charge of their health and make positive changes in their lives is something Helen intends to do with her cookbook. She is aware personally of how difficult it may be to overcome bad habits, but she also understands that everything is achievable with the correct tools and attitude.

Chapter 1: What you need to know about fatty liver disease

Hepatic steatosis, another name for the illness known as fatty liver disease, is characterised by an abnormal buildup of fat in the liver cells. The liver is a crucial organ that performs a number of vital bodily processes, including the detoxification of dangerous chemicals, the production of bile to break down lipids, and the storage of glucose as glycogen for energy. Extra fat in the liver might prevent it from doing its usual tasks, causing damage to the organ and other problems with health. Our discussion of the causes, signs, symptoms, diagnosis, therapy, and prevention of fatty liver disease will take place in this chapter.

Types of Fatty Liver Disease

There are two main types of fatty liver disease: non-alcoholic fatty liver disease (NAFLD) and alcoholic fatty liver disease (AFLD).

Non-Alcoholic Fatty Liver Disease:

The most prevalent form of fatty liver disease, NAFLD, affects a sizable portion of the world's population. In persons who do not drink excessive amounts of alcohol, it is characterised by the buildup of extra fat in the liver cells. Non-alcoholic steatohepatitis (NASH), a more severe type of the illness that is linked to inflammation and liver damage, can develop from NAFLD. Cirrhosis, liver failure, and liver cancer can result from NASH.

Alcoholic Fatty Liver Disease:

Alcoholism is the primary cause of AFLD because it causes the liver cells to accumulate fat. Alcohol is metabolised in the liver, and overindulging puts the liver under too much stress and reduces its efficiency. A condition known as alcoholic hepatitis, which is marked by inflammation and liver damage, can develop from AFLD. Cirrhosis, liver failure, and liver cancer are further complications of alcoholic hepatitis.

Causes of Fatty Liver Disease

Insulin resistance, which causes a buildup of fat in the liver cells, is the main contributor of NAFLD. Obesity, type 2 diabetes, metabolic syndrome, and elevated triglyceride levels in the blood are all linked to insulin resistance. Other variables that increase the chance of developing NAFLD include a sedentary lifestyle, a diet heavy in fat and sugar, and certain medical diseases including hypothyroidism and polycystic ovarian syndrome.

Alcoholism in excess is the main contributor of AFLD. The quantity of alcohol that might cause AFLD varies from person to person and depends on a number of variables, including heredity, sex, age, and general health.

Symptoms of Fatty Liver Disease:

Early-stage fatty liver disease may go undetected and only be discovered by normal blood testing or imaging procedures like ultrasounds. However, if the illness worsens, the following signs and symptoms might appear:

Fatigue

Abdominal discomfort

Jaundice (yellowing of the skin and eyes)

Swelling in the legs and abdomen

Loss of appetite

Unintentional weight loss

Nausea and vomiting

Confusion and difficulty concentrating

Spider-like blood vessels on the skin

Enlarged liver

Diagnosis of Fatty Liver Disease

Blood tests, imaging studies, and liver biopsies are frequently used to identify fatty liver disease.

Elevated levels of liver enzymes, which signify liver inflammation or injury, can be found by blood testing. The presence of fat in the liver may be detected, and the degree of liver damage can be assessed, using imaging techniques including ultrasound, CT scan, and MRI. During a liver biopsy, a tiny sample of liver tissue is removed to be examined under a microscope to assess the degree of liver damage and the presence of inflammation or scarring.

Treatment of Fatty Liver Disease

Numerous conditions, such as obesity, diabetes, high cholesterol, and binge drinking, can result in fatty liver. Fatty liver disease can cause major liver damage, such as cirrhosis or liver cancer, if it is not addressed. Thankfully, there are a number of therapies for fatty liver disease that can aid in halting or even reversing the illness's course.

Taking care of the underlying cause is the first step in treating fatty liver disease. For instance, weight loss through diet and exercise is frequently advised if the disease is brought on by obesity. This can enhance liver function and help lower the amount of fat in the liver. A nutritious diet that is high in fibre, low in saturated and trans fats, and abundant in fruits and vegetables can also be advantageous. Additionally, as alcohol usage can aggravate fatty liver disease, patients can be recommended to cut back or stop drinking.

A number of drugs may be recommended in addition to lifestyle modifications to treat fatty liver disease. These drugs act by lowering liver inflammation or by lowering the amount of fat that is stored in the liver cells. Pioglitazone, vitamin E, and ursodeoxycholic acid are a few typical drugs used to treat fatty liver disease. It is crucial to remember that not all individuals with fatty liver disease will require medication, thus the choice to do so should be based on each individual circumstance.

Imaging studies or treatments like liver biopsies may be suggested for patients with more severe fatty liver disease. These examinations can aid in estimating the degree of liver damage and aid in making treatment recommendations. If the liver damage is severe and permanent, liver transplantation may occasionally be required.

There are a number of herbal therapies that may be used in conjunction with modern procedures to treat fatty liver disease. For instance, studies have demonstrated the anti-inflammatory and antioxidant qualities of several herbs and supplements, including milk thistle, dandelion root, and turmeric, which can help to preserve the liver and enhance liver function. Natural remedies should not be used in place of medical care, it is crucial to remember, and patients should always speak with their doctor before beginning any new supplements or herbal medicines.

Finally, it's crucial to remember that the best way to cure fatty liver disease is frequently through lifestyle modifications. Maintaining a healthy weight, eating a balanced diet, getting regular exercise, and abstaining from alcohol can all assist the liver function and limit the disease's progression. Patients with fatty liver disease should consult with their doctor frequently to create a thorough treatment strategy that tackles both the underlying cause of the condition and any possible side effects. Many people with fatty liver disease can successfully control their illness and prevent significant liver damage with the correct treatment strategy.

Foods to eat for healthy liver

One of our body's most vital organs, the liver is in charge of digesting and getting rid of toxins, making bile for digestion, and storing energy in the form of glycogen. A balanced diet is one of the greatest methods to maintain a healthy liver, which is crucial for our overall health and wellness.

Leafy greens

Leafy greens are a great source of vitamins and minerals that are vital for the health of the liver. Examples include spinach, kale and rocket. Antioxidants included in these greens can shield the liver from harm brought on by free radicals, which are naturally created by the body as part of the metabolic process. Leafy greens also contain a lot of chlorophyll, a vitamin that aids in liver detoxification.

Cruciferous vegetables

Cruciferous vegetables like broccoli, cauliflower, and Brussels sprouts are also excellent for the health of the liver. These veggies include a substance known as sulforaphane, which has been demonstrated to shield the liver from harm brought on by toxins. Additionally, cruciferous vegetables have a high fibre content, which may aid in better digestion and support a balanced gut microbiota.

Fatty fish

Omega-3 fatty acids are found in abundance in fatty fish like salmon, mackerel, and sardines and have been demonstrated to decrease inflammation and enhance liver function. A strong source of vitamin D, which helps lower the risk of liver disease, is also found in fatty fish.

Nuts and seeds

Another excellent food for liver health is nuts and seeds, such as chia seeds, almonds, and walnuts. Antioxidants found in abundance in these foods can aid in defending the liver from damage brought on by free radicals. Nuts and seeds are also a fantastic source of healthy fats, which can lower inflammation and raise cholesterol.

Berries

Antioxidants, which can help prevent liver damage, are abundant in berries including blueberries, raspberries, and strawberries. Berries also have a high fibre content, which can aid in better digestion and support a balanced gut microbiota.

Garlic

Due to its high allicin concentration, which has been demonstrated to shield the liver against toxicity-related harm, garlic is a potent diet for liver health. Additionally, the anti-inflammatory effects of garlic can help lessen liver inflammation.

Olive oil

Olive oil is a fantastic source of healthy fats that can help lower inflammation and raise cholesterol levels. Olive oil also has antioxidants that may aid in defending the liver against oxidative stress.

Green tea

Green tea is a fantastic beverage for liver health because it contains a lot of catechins, an antioxidant that can help shield the liver from harm brought on by pollutants. The anti-inflammatory qualities of green tea can also aid to lessen liver inflammation.

Turmeric

For its therapeutic characteristics, the spice turmeric has been used for thousands of years. It has been demonstrated that the substance curcumin in it can shield the liver from harm brought on by pollutants. In addition, curcumin contains anti-inflammatory effects that may help lessen liver inflammation.

Citrus fruits

Vitamin C, a potent antioxidant that can aid in protecting the liver from damage brought on by free radicals, is abundant in citrus fruits like oranges, grapefruits, and lemons. Citrus fruits are also an excellent source of fibre, which helps enhance digestion and support a healthy gut microbiota.

A balanced diet is one of the greatest methods to maintain a healthy liver, which is crucial for our overall health and wellness.

Foods you should avoid when you have fatty liver

Diet has a significant impact on FLD development and progression, and specific foods should be avoided to successfully treat the illness. The foods that should be avoided for fatty liver are covered in this chapter.

Meals rich in calories and sugar

People with fatty liver disease need to stay away from foods that are heavy in sugar and calories. This covers sweetened beverages including soda, fruit juice, and energy drinks. These beverages can cause weight gain since they are high in calories and sugar, which is a risk factor for FLD. Also to be avoided are high-calorie items such as processed snacks, sweets, and fast food. Instead, those who have FLD should concentrate on eating nutrient-dense, low-calorie meals like fruits, vegetables, and lean meats.

Alcohol

Alcohol is a significant cause of FLD and other liver diseases. Alcohol intake can raise liver fat levels and promote inflammation, both of which can harm the liver. All types of alcohol should be avoided by those with FLD, including beer, wine, and spirits. It is important to remember that alcohol use, even in moderation, can cause liver damage.

Fried foods

People with FLD should stay away from fried meals that are rich in fat and calories, such as french fries, fried chicken, and onion rings. These meals can exacerbate the problem by causing weight gain and by putting more fat in the liver. Those who have FLD should pick healthier cooking techniques instead, such baking, grilling, or steaming.

Processed foods

Processed foods should be avoided by persons with FLD since they are frequently rich in sugar, salt, and harmful fats. Along with frozen meals, processed meats like bacon, sausage and hot dogs are also included. These meals can lead to weight gain and raise your chance of getting FLD. Instead, those who have FLD should pick full, minimally processed meals such fruits, vegetables, whole grains, and lean meats that are in their natural state.

Lactose-rich dairy products

People with FLD should refrain from consuming high-fat dairy products including cheese, cream, and whole milk. These goods contain a lot of saturated fat, which can lead to weight gain and raise liver fat levels. Instead, those who suffer from FLD ought to pick low-fat or fat-free dairy items like skim milk, low-fat yoghurt, and reduced-fat cheese.

Carbs that have been refined

People with FLD should avoid refined carbohydrates including white bread, white rice, and pasta. These meals include a lot of sugar, which can lead to weight gain and increase liver fat. Instead, those who have FLD should pick whole grains that are high in fibre and can help control blood sugar levels, such brown rice, quinoa, and whole wheat bread.

Trans fat

Processed foods including baked products, snack foods, and fried meals contain trans fats, a kind of harmful fat. These fats can cause weight gain and raise liver fat levels, which can exacerbate FLD. Food labels must be examined carefully, and trans-fat-containing goods must be avoided. As an alternative, those who have FLD can pick foods high in healthy fats such avocados, nuts, seeds, and fatty fish.

Sodium-rich foods

People with FLD should stay away from high-sodium meals such canned soups, processed meats, and salty snacks. When consumed in excess, these foods can make FLD worse.

How air fryer can benefit fatty liver patient

As a healthier alternative to conventional deep fryers, air fryers have grown in popularity over the past several years. Instead of using oil to cook food, air fryers use hot air, producing tasty food that is crispy and low in fat and calories. An air fryer can be a helpful tool for persons with fatty liver disease (FLD) to help control the illness. I'll talk about how air fryers can help persons with FLD.

Lower fat intake

The fact that the amount of fat in the dish is greatly reduced when using an air fryer is one of its key advantages. Traditional deep frying calls for a substantial amount of oil, which can lead to weight gain and increase liver fat. Air frying, on the other hand, uses little to no oil and produces a lower-fat version of the same dish. For instance, deep-fried chicken wings can have up to 20 grammes of fat per serving, but air-fried wings only have 5 grammes.

Reduced calorie intake

Using an air fryer can lower calorie consumption in addition to lowering fat intake. Since little to no oil is used in air frying, the meal has much fewer calories than conventional deep-fried cuisine. For instance, whereas air-fried French fries only have 150 calories per serving, a portion of deep-fried French fries has about 365 calories. People with FLD can control their weight and lessen the amount of fat in their livers by consuming less calories.

Healthier cooking method

A healthier alternative to conventional deep frying is air frying. Food that has been deep-fried is immersed in hot oil, which can cause the development of dangerous substances including acrylamide and polycyclic aromatic hydrocarbons (PAHs). These substances have been connected to a higher risk of cancer and other illnesses. In contrast, air frying cooks food using hot air, which produces less carcinogens and makes for a healthier supper.

Versatility

Due to its adaptability, air fryers may be used to cook a variety of items, such as chicken, fish, vegetables, and even desserts. This makes it simple for those who have FLD to produce flavorful yet healthful meals at home.

Additionally, air fryers are simple to operate and use little to no oil, making it easier to prepare nutritious meals at home.

Time-saving

Time may be saved in the kitchen by using an air fryer. Because air fryers cook food more quickly than conventional ovens and deep fryers, meals may be made swiftly and simply. For those with FLD who may have limited energy or movement, this can be extremely beneficial.

Cost-effective

Over time, air fryers are also less expensive. An air fryer may cost more up front than a conventional deep fryer or oven, but over time it will cost less since it consumes less electricity and oil. Cooking at home is also typically less expensive than dining out, which can be advantageous for those with FLD who need to control their spending.

More control over ingredients

People with FLD can have more control over the ingredients used in their cuisine by preparing meals at home in an air fryer. As a result, individuals are able to stay away from bad fats, too much salt, and other elements that might aggravate their illness. Instead, they can utilise healthy fats that have been proven to improve liver function, including olive oil or avocado oil.

For those with fatty liver disease, air fryers might be a useful tool. Air fryers can assist persons with FLD manage their disease and enhance their quality of life by decreasing fat and calorie consumption, utilising a healthier cooking method, and offering variety and time-saving advantages.

Chapter 2: Breakfast recipes

Recipe 1: Air Fryer Oatmeal

Cooking time: 10 minutes

Prep time: 5 minutes

Servings: 2

Ingredients:

1 cup rolled oats

1/2 cup water

1/2 cup milk of choice (almond, soy, oat, etc.)

1/2 teaspoon cinnamon

1/4 teaspoon nutmeg

1/4 teaspoon salt

1 tablespoon honey or maple syrup (optional)

Instructions:

In a bowl, combine oats, water, milk, cinnamon, nutmeg, and salt.

Stir until well combined.

Pour mixture into the air fryer basket.

Cook at 350 degrees F for 10 minutes, or until oats are cooked through.

Stir in honey or maple syrup (if desired).

Serve immediately.

Nutrition information (per serving):

Calories: 250

Fat: 4 grams

Saturated fat: 1 gram

Cholesterol: 15 milligrams

Sodium: 150 milligrams

Carbohydrates: 45 grams

Fiber: 4 grams

Sugar: 15 grams

Protein: 10 grams

Recipe 2: Air Fryer Egg White Frittata

Cooking time: 15 minutes

Prep time: 5 minutes

Servings: 2

Ingredients:

6 egg whites

1/2 cup shredded cheese (cheddar, mozzarella, etc.)

1/2 cup chopped vegetables (spinach, mushrooms, onions, etc.)

1/4 teaspoon salt

1/4 teaspoon black pepper

Instructions:

In a bowl, whisk together egg whites, cheese, vegetables, salt, and pepper.

Pour mixture into the air fryer basket.

Cook at 350 degrees F for 15 minutes, or until egg whites are set.

Serve immediately.

Nutrition information (per serving):

Calories: 170

Fat: 10 grams

Saturated fat: 4 grams

Cholesterol: 15 milligrams

Sodium: 200 milligrams

Carbohydrates: 3 grams

Fiber: 1 gram

Sugar: 1 gram

Protein: 25 grams

Recipe 3: Air Fryer Yogurt Parfait

Cooking time: 0 minutes

Prep time: 5 minutes

Servings: 1

Ingredients:

1 cup plain yogurt

1/2 cup granola

1/4 cup berries (blueberries, raspberries, strawberries, etc.)

1 tablespoon honey or maple syrup (optional)

Instructions:

In a glass or bowl, layer yogurt, granola, berries, and honey or maple syrup (if desired).

Enjoy immediately.

Nutrition information (per serving):

Calories: 300

Fat: 10 grams

Saturated fat: 3 grams

Cholesterol: 25 milligrams

Sodium: 150 milligrams

Carbohydrates: 45 grams

Fiber: 4 grams

Sugar: 25 grams

Protein: 15 grams

Recipe 4: Air Fryer Egg White Omelet

Cooking time: 10 minutes

Prep time: 5 minutes

Servings: 2

Ingredients:

6 egg whites

1/2 cup vegetables (chopped)

1/4 cup cheese (shredded)

Salt and pepper to taste

Instructions:

In a bowl, whisk together the egg whites, vegetables, cheese, salt, and pepper.

Pour the mixture into the air fryer basket.

Cook at 350 degrees Fahrenheit for 10 minutes, or until the eggs are cooked through.

Serve immediately.

Nutrition:

Calories: 150

Fat: 5 grams

Saturated fat: 1 gram

Cholesterol: 0 milligrams

Sodium: 150 milligrams

Carbohydrates: 4 grams

Fiber: 1 gram

Sugar: 1 gram

Protein: 20 grams

Recipe 5: Air Fryer Breakfast Sandwich

Cooking time: 10 minutes

Prep time: 5 minutes

Servings: 1

Ingredients:

1 English muffin

1 egg

1 slice cheese

1 slice ham

1 tablespoon butter

Salt and pepper to taste

Instructions:

Split the English muffin in half.

In a small bowl, whisk together the egg.

In the air fryer basket, place the English muffin halves, cheese, ham, and egg.

Dot the top of the egg with butter.

Season with salt and pepper to taste.

Cook at 350 degrees Fahrenheit for 10 minutes, or until the egg is cooked through.

Serve immediately.

Nutrition:

Calories: 300

Fat: 15 grams

Saturated fat: 5 grams

Cholesterol: 200 milligrams

Sodium: 600 milligrams

Carbohydrates: 25 grams

Fiber: 2 grams

Sugar: 5 grams

Protein: 15 grams

Recipe 6: Air Fryer Breakfast Sausage Patties

Cooking time: 10 minutes

Prep time: 5 minutes

Servings: 2

Ingredients:

1 pound breakfast sausage

1/4 cup bread crumbs

1/4 cup grated Parmesan cheese

1 egg, beaten

1 teaspoon salt

1/2 teaspoon black pepper

Instructions:

Preheat the air fryer to 350 degrees Fahrenheit.

In a bowl, combine the sausage, bread crumbs, Parmesan cheese, egg, salt, and pepper.

Mix well to combine.

Form the mixture into 4 patties.

Place the patties in the air fryer basket.

Cook for 10 minutes, or until the patties are cooked through.

Serve immediately.

Nutrition:

Calories: 250

Fat: 15 grams

Saturated fat: 5 grams

Cholesterol: 40 milligrams

Sodium: 500 milligrams

Carbohydrates: 10 grams

Fiber: 1 gram

Sugar: 1 gram

Protein: 15 grams

Recipe 7: Air Fryer Omelette

Cooking Time: 10 minutes

Prep Time: 5 minutes

Servings: 2

Ingredients:

4 large eggs

1/4 cup diced bell pepper

1/4 cup diced onion

1/4 cup diced tomato

1/4 cup shredded low-fat cheese

Salt and pepper to taste

Instructions:

Preheat the air fryer to 350°F.

In a mixing bowl, beat the eggs until smooth.

Add the diced bell pepper, onion, and tomato to the bowl and mix well.

Season the mixture with salt and pepper to taste.

Pour the mixture into the air fryer basket and sprinkle the shredded cheese on top.

Cook for 10 minutes or until the omelette is set and the cheese is melted.

Serve hot.

Nutrition per serving:

Calories: 183kcal

Fat: 12g

Carbohydrates: 4g

Protein: 15g

Sodium: 275mg

Recipe 8: Air Fryer Breakfast Potatoes

Cooking Time: 20 minutes

Prep Time: 10 minutes

Servings: 2

Ingredients:

2 medium-sized potatoes, washed and chopped into small pieces

1 tablespoon olive oil

1/2 teaspoon garlic powder

1/2 teaspoon onion powder

Salt and pepper to taste

Instructions:

Preheat the air fryer to 375°F.

In a mixing bowl, toss the chopped potatoes with olive oil, garlic powder, onion powder, salt, and pepper.

Place the seasoned potatoes into the air fryer basket and cook for 20 minutes, or until they are crispy and golden brown.

Serve hot.

Nutrition per serving:

Calories: 136kcal

Fat: 4g

Carbohydrates: 23g

Protein: 3g

Sodium: 33mg

Recipe 9: Air Fryer Avocado and Egg Breakfast

Prep Time: 5 minutes

Cook Time: 8-10 minutes

Servings: 2

Ingredients:

1 avocado, halved and pitted

2 eggs

Salt and pepper, to taste

Chopped fresh parsley, for garnish (optional)

Instructions:

Preheat the air fryer to 350°F (175°C).

Scoop out a little bit of the avocado flesh from each half to make room for the egg.

Crack an egg into each avocado half.

Sprinkle with salt and pepper.

Place the avocado halves in the air fryer basket.

Cook for 8-10 minutes or until the egg whites are set.

Garnish with chopped parsley if desired.

Nutritional Information (per serving):

Calories: 233

Protein: 9g

Fat: 20g

Carbohydrates: 9g

Fiber: 7g

Sugar: 0.8g

Sodium: 67mg

Recipe 10: Air Fryer Sweet Potato Hash

Prep Time: 10 minutes

Cook Time: 15-20 minutes

Servings: 4

Ingredients:

2 medium sweet potatoes, peeled and diced

1 red bell pepper, diced

1 yellow onion, diced

2 cloves garlic, minced

2 tablespoons olive oil

1 teaspoon smoked paprika

1 teaspoon ground cumin

Salt and pepper, to taste

4 large eggs

Chopped fresh cilantro, for garnish (optional)

Instructions:

Preheat the air fryer to 375°F (190°C).

In a large bowl, toss together the sweet potatoes, bell pepper, onion, garlic, olive oil, smoked paprika, cumin, salt, and pepper.

Spread the mixture in a single layer in the air fryer basket.

Cook for 15-20 minutes or until the sweet potatoes are tender and golden brown, stirring once or twice during cooking.

Crack an egg on top of each serving of sweet potato hash.

Cook for an additional 5-6 minutes or until the eggs are cooked to your liking.

Garnish with chopped cilantro if desired.

Nutritional Information (per serving):

Calories: 270

Protein: 7g

Fat: 13g

Carbohydrates: 31g

Fiber: 6g

Sugar: 8g

Sodium: 170mg

Chapter 3: Lunch recipes

Recipe 1: Air Fryer Salmon with Roasted Vegetables

Prep Time: 10 minutes

Cook Time: 15 minutes

Servings: 2

Ingredients:

2 salmon fillets (6 ounces each)

2 cups mixed vegetables (such as broccoli, zucchini, and bell pepper)

2 tablespoons olive oil

1 teaspoon garlic powder

1 teaspoon dried thyme

Salt and black pepper to taste

Instructions:

Preheat the air fryer to 400°F.

Cut the mixed vegetables into bite-sized pieces.

Season the salmon fillets with garlic powder, thyme, salt, and black pepper.

Drizzle the vegetables with olive oil and season with salt and black pepper.

Place the salmon fillets and vegetables in the air fryer basket, making sure they are not crowded.

Cook for 10 minutes, then flip the salmon and vegetables.

Cook for another 5 minutes, or until the salmon is cooked through and the vegetables are tender.

Serve immediately.

Nutrition Information per serving:

Calories: 356

Total Fat: 23g

Saturated Fat: 4g

Cholesterol: 85mg

Sodium: 120mg

Total Carbohydrates: 8g

Dietary Fiber: 3g

Sugar: 3g

Protein: 30g

Recipe 2: Air Fryer Turkey Burgers with Sweet Potato Fries

Prep Time: 15 minutes

Cook Time: 20 minutes

Servings: 2

Ingredients:

1 pound ground turkey

1 egg

1/2 cup breadcrumbs

1 teaspoon garlic powder

1 teaspoon onion powder

Salt and black pepper to taste

2 small sweet potatoes

1 tablespoon olive oil

Salt and black pepper to taste

Instructions:

Preheat the air fryer to 375°F.

Peel the sweet potatoes and cut them into thin fries.

Toss the sweet potato fries with olive oil, salt, and black pepper.

In a bowl, mix the ground turkey, egg, breadcrumbs, garlic powder, onion powder, salt, and black pepper.

Form the turkey mixture into two patties.

Place the sweet potato fries in the air fryer basket and cook for 10 minutes.

Add the turkey burgers to the air fryer basket and cook for another 10 minutes, or until the burgers are cooked through.

Serve immediately.

Nutrition Information per serving:

Calories: 478

Total Fat: 22g

Saturated Fat: 4g

Cholesterol: 223mg

Sodium: 476mg

Total Carbohydrates: 36g

Dietary Fiber: 5g

Sugar: 7g

Protein: 37g

Recipe 3: Air Fryer Chicken Tenders with Sweet Potato Fries

Cooking time: 25 minutes

Prep time: 15 minutes

Servings: 2

Ingredients:

2 boneless, skinless chicken breasts, cut into strips

1 large sweet potato, cut into fries

1 tablespoon olive oil

1 teaspoon paprika

1/2 teaspoon garlic powder

Salt and pepper to taste

Instructions:

Preheat your air fryer to 400°F.

Toss the sweet potato fries with olive oil, paprika, garlic powder, salt, and pepper.

Place the chicken strips and the sweet potato fries in the air fryer basket.

Cook for 20-25 minutes, flipping the chicken strips and the sweet potato fries halfway through, until the chicken is cooked through and the sweet potato fries are crispy.

Serve hot.

Nutrition per serving:

Calories: 400

Fat: 12g

Protein: 36g

Carbohydrates: 34g

Fiber: 5g

Recipe 4: Air Fryer Tofu with Broccoli and Brown Rice

Cooking time: 20 minutes

Prep time: 10 minutes

Servings: 2

Ingredients:

1 block extra-firm tofu, pressed and cut into cubes

1 head broccoli, cut into florets

1 tablespoon olive oil

1 teaspoon soy sauce

1/2 teaspoon garlic powder

Salt and pepper to taste

1 cup cooked brown rice

Instructions:

Preheat your air fryer to 375°F.

Toss the tofu and broccoli with olive oil, soy sauce, garlic powder, salt, and pepper.

Place the tofu and broccoli in the air fryer basket.

Cook for 15-20 minutes, shaking the basket halfway through, until the tofu is crispy and the broccoli is tender.

Serve with cooked brown rice.

Nutrition per serving:

Calories: 270

Fat: 12g

Protein: 13g

Carbohydrates: 30g

Fiber: 6g

Recipe 5: Air Fryer Chicken Salad
Cooking Time: 20 minutes

Prep Time: 10 minutes

Servings: 2

Ingredients:

2 boneless, skinless chicken breasts

2 cups mixed greens

1 medium avocado, diced

1 medium tomato, diced

1/4 cup diced red onion

2 tbsp chopped fresh cilantro

1 tbsp olive oil

1 tbsp lime juice

Salt and pepper to taste

Instructions:

Preheat the air fryer to 375°F.

Season the chicken breasts with salt and pepper, and place them in the air fryer basket. Cook for 20 minutes or until the chicken is cooked through.

In a large bowl, combine the mixed greens, avocado, tomato, red onion, and cilantro.

In a small bowl, whisk together the olive oil, lime juice, salt, and pepper to make the dressing.

Slice the chicken and add it to the salad. Drizzle the dressing over the salad and toss to combine.

Nutrition Information (per serving):

Calories: 365

Total Fat: 20g

Saturated Fat: 3g

Cholesterol: 85mg

Sodium: 205mg

Total Carbohydrates: 14g

Dietary Fiber: 8g

Sugar: 2g

Protein: 35g

Recipe 6: Air Fryer Salmon with Lemon and Dill

Cooking Time: 10 minutes

Prep Time: 10 minutes

Servings: 2

Ingredients:

2 salmon fillets (6 ounces each)

1 tablespoon of olive oil

1 teaspoon of dried dill

Salt and pepper to taste

1 lemon, sliced

Instructions:

Preheat the air fryer to 400°F.

Brush the salmon fillets with olive oil and season them with dill, salt, and pepper.

Place the salmon fillets in the air fryer basket and top them with lemon slices.

Cook the salmon for 8-10 minutes until it is cooked through and flakes easily with a fork.

Once done, remove the salmon from the air fryer and let it rest for 5 minutes before serving.

Nutrition (per serving):

Calories: 311

Protein: 36g

Fat: 16g

Carbohydrates: 2g

Fiber: 1g

Sugar: 1g

Sodium: 190mg

Recipe 7: Air Fryer Sweet Potato Fries

Cooking Time: 20 minutes

Prep Time: 15 minutes

Servings: 2

Ingredients:

2 medium sweet potatoes, peeled and cut into fries

1 tablespoon of olive oil

1 teaspoon of paprika

1/2 teaspoon of garlic powder

Salt and pepper to taste

Instructions:

Preheat the air fryer to 400°F.

Toss the sweet potato fries with olive oil, paprika, garlic powder, salt, and pepper.

Place the sweet potato fries in the air fryer basket and cook for 15-20 minutes, shaking the basket occasionally to ensure even cooking.

Once done, remove the sweet potato fries from the air fryer and serve immediately.

Nutrition (per serving):

Calories: 183

Protein: 2g

Fat: 7g

Carbohydrates: 30g

Fiber: 4g

Sugar: 6g

Sodium: 121mg

Recipe 8: Air Fryer Chicken Breast with Quinoa and Vegetables

Cooking Time: 20 minutes

Prep Time: 10 minutes

Servings: 2

Ingredients:

2 boneless, skinless chicken breasts

1 tbsp olive oil

Salt and pepper, to taste

1/2 cup quinoa

1 cup low-sodium chicken broth

1 small zucchini, sliced

1 small yellow squash, sliced

1/2 red bell pepper, sliced

1/2 yellow bell pepper, sliced

Instructions:

Preheat the air fryer to 400°F.

Brush the chicken breasts with olive oil and season with salt and pepper.

In a small pot, combine the quinoa and chicken broth and bring to a boil. Reduce the heat and simmer for 15-20 minutes or until the quinoa is cooked through.

Arrange the sliced vegetables in the air fryer basket.

Place the chicken breasts on top of the vegetables in the air fryer basket.

Air fry for 20 minutes or until the chicken is cooked through.

Serve hot with quinoa.

Nutrition per serving:

Calories: 370

Fat: 11g

Carbohydrates: 29g

Protein: 38g

Recipe 9: Air Fryer Fish and Chips

Cooking Time: 15-20 minutes

Prep Time: 10 minutes

Servings: 2

Ingredients:

2 fillets of white fish (such as cod or haddock)

2 medium-sized potatoes

1 tablespoon olive oil

1/4 teaspoon garlic powder

1/4 teaspoon paprika

Salt and pepper, to taste

Instructions:

Preheat the air fryer to 400°F.

Peel and slice the potatoes into thin rounds.

Toss the potato slices with the olive oil, garlic powder, paprika, salt, and pepper.

Place the potato slices in the air fryer basket and cook for 10-12 minutes, or until they are crispy and golden brown.

Season the fish fillets with salt and pepper.

Place the fish fillets in the air fryer basket and cook for 5-8 minutes, or until they are cooked through and crispy.

Serve the fish and chips together, with a side salad if desired.

Nutrition Information per Serving:

Calories: 371kcal | Fat: 10g | Saturated Fat: 2g | Cholesterol: 63mg | Sodium: 85mg | Potassium: 1226mg | Carbohydrates: 43g | Fiber: 6g | Sugar: 2g | Protein: 27g | Vitamin A: 237IU | Vitamin C: 34mg | Calcium: 74mg | Iron: 3mg

Recipe 10: Air Fryer Chicken Fajitas

Cooking Time: 15-20 minutes

Prep Time: 10 minutes

Servings: 2

Ingredients:

2 boneless, skinless chicken breasts, sliced

1 bell pepper, sliced

1 onion, sliced

1 tablespoon olive oil

1 teaspoon chili powder

1/2 teaspoon cumin

1/4 teaspoon garlic powder

Salt and pepper, to taste

Juice of 1 lime

Instructions:

Preheat the air fryer to 400°F.

In a small bowl, mix together the olive oil, chili powder, cumin, garlic powder, salt, pepper, and lime juice.

Add the chicken, bell pepper, and onion to the bowl and toss to coat.

Place the chicken, bell pepper, and onion in the air fryer basket and cook for 12-15 minutes, or until the chicken is cooked through and the vegetables are tender.

Serve the chicken fajitas with whole grain tortillas, avocado, and salsa.

Nutrition Information per Serving:

Calories: 319kcal | Fat: 13g | Saturated Fat: 2g | Cholesterol: 108mg | Sodium: 189mg | Potassium: 939mg | Carbohydrates: 15g | Fiber: 4g | Sugar: 6g | Protein: 34g | Vitamin A: 1966IU | Vitamin C: 76mg | Calcium: 43mg | Iron: 2mg

Chapter 4: Dinner recipes

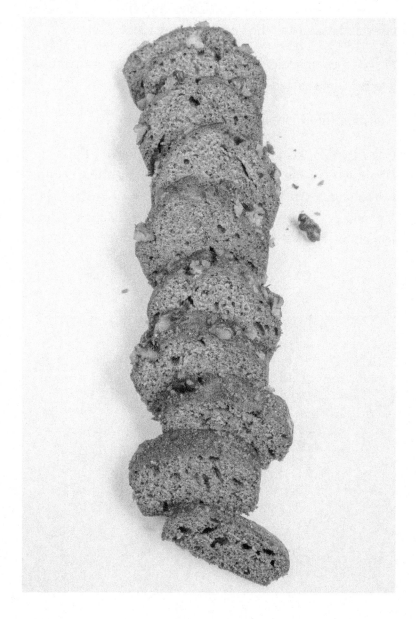

Recipe 1: Air Fried Salmon with Asparagus

Cooking time: 12 minutes

Prep time: 10 minutes

Servings: 2

Ingredients:

2 salmon fillets

1 bunch of asparagus

1 tbsp olive oil

1 tsp garlic powder

1 tsp salt

1/2 tsp black pepper

Instructions:

Preheat the air fryer to 400°F.

Rinse and pat dry the salmon fillets and asparagus.

Drizzle olive oil over the salmon fillets and sprinkle with garlic powder, salt, and black pepper. Rub to coat the salmon well.

Place the salmon fillets in the air fryer basket and add the asparagus around the salmon.

Air fry for 12 minutes, flipping the asparagus halfway through.

Serve the air fried salmon with the asparagus.

Nutrition per serving:

Calories: 339

Fat: 19g

Saturated Fat: 3g

Cholesterol: 94mg

Sodium: 685mg

Carbohydrates: 5g

Fiber: 2g

Sugar: 2g

Protein: 35g

Recipe 2: Air Fried Chicken with Roasted Vegetables

Cooking time: 20 minutes

Prep time: 15 minutes

Servings: 4

Ingredients:

4 chicken breasts

2 cups broccoli florets

2 cups cauliflower florets

2 tbsp olive oil

1 tsp garlic powder

1 tsp paprika

1 tsp salt

1/2 tsp black pepper

Instructions:

Preheat the air fryer to 400°F.

Rinse and pat dry the chicken breasts and vegetables.

Drizzle olive oil over the vegetables and sprinkle with garlic powder, paprika, salt, and black pepper. Toss to coat well.

Rub the chicken breasts with the same seasoning mixture.

Place the chicken breasts in the air fryer basket and add the seasoned vegetables around the chicken.

Air fry for 20 minutes, flipping the vegetables halfway through.

Serve the air fried chicken with the roasted vegetables.

Nutrition per serving:

Calories: 296

Fat: 11g

Saturated Fat: 2g

Cholesterol: 98mg

Sodium: 707mg

Carbohydrates: 10g

Fiber: 4g

Sugar: 3g

Protein: 39g

Recipe 3: Air Fried Shrimp Tacos

Cooking time: 10 minutes

Prep time: 15 minutes

Servings: 4

Ingredients:

1 lb large shrimp, peeled and deveined

1 tbsp olive oil

1 tsp chili powder

1 tsp paprika

1/2 tsp cumin

1/2 tsp garlic powder

1/2 tsp salt

1/4 tsp black pepper

8 small corn tortillas

2 cups shredded cabbage

1 avocado, sliced

1 lime, cut into wedges

Instructions:

Preheat the air fryer to 400°F.

Rinse and pat dry the shrimp.

In a small bowl, mix together olive oil, chili powder, paprika, cumin, garlic powder, salt, and black pepper.

Add the shrimp to the seasoning mixture and toss to coat.

Place the shrimp in the air fryer basket and air fry for 5-6 minutes, flipping the shrimp halfway through.

Recipe 4: Air Fryer Chicken Breast with Broccoli
Cooking time: 18-20 minutes

Prep time: 5 minutes

Servings: 2

Ingredients:

2 boneless, skinless chicken breasts

1 head of broccoli

1 tablespoon olive oil

1/2 teaspoon paprika

Salt and pepper to taste

Instructions:

Preheat the air fryer to 375°F.

Rinse and pat dry the chicken breasts and broccoli.

In a small bowl, mix the olive oil, paprika, salt, and pepper.

Brush the olive oil mixture over the chicken breasts and broccoli.

Place the chicken breasts and broccoli in the air fryer basket.

Cook for 18-20 minutes or until the chicken is cooked through and the broccoli is tender.

Serve immediately.

Nutrition per serving:

Calories: 270

Total Fat: 11g

Saturated Fat: 2g

Cholesterol: 102mg

Sodium: 159mg

Total Carbohydrates: 7g

Dietary Fiber: 3g

Protein: 35g

Recipe 5: Air Fryer Pork Chops with Brussels Sprouts

Cooking time: 15-20 minutes

Prep time: 5 minutes

Servings: 2

Ingredients:

2 pork chops

1 pound Brussels sprouts

1 tablespoon olive oil

1/2 teaspoon dried thyme

Salt and pepper to taste

Instructions:

Preheat the air fryer to 375°F.

Rinse and pat dry the pork chops and Brussels sprouts.

In a small bowl, mix the olive oil, thyme, salt, and pepper.

Brush the olive oil mixture over the pork chops and Brussels sprouts.

Place the pork chops and Brussels sprouts in the air fryer basket.

Cook for 15-20 minutes or until the pork is cooked through and the Brussels sprouts are tender.

Serve immediately.

Nutrition per serving:

Calories: 351

Total Fat: 15g

Saturated Fat: 4g

Cholesterol: 98mg

Sodium: 113mg

Total Carbohydrates: 19g

Recipe 6: Air Fryer Turkey Meatballs with Marinara Sauce

Cooking Time: 15 minutes

Prep Time: 10 minutes

Servings: 4

Ingredients:

1 lb ground turkey

1 egg

1/2 cup breadcrumbs

1/4 cup grated Parmesan cheese

2 garlic cloves, minced

1 tsp dried basil

1 tsp dried oregano

Salt and pepper to taste

1 cup marinara sauce

Instructions:

Preheat the air fryer to 375°F.

In a bowl, mix the ground turkey, egg, breadcrumbs, Parmesan cheese, garlic, basil, oregano, salt, and pepper.

Shape the mixture into 16 meatballs.

Place the meatballs in the air fryer basket and air fry for 15 minutes, or until they are cooked through.

Heat the marinara sauce in a small saucepan or in the microwave.

Serve the meatballs with the marinara sauce on top.

Nutritional Information per serving (4 meatballs with sauce):

Calories: 284 kcal

Total Fat: 11g

Saturated Fat: 3g

Carbohydrates: 15g

Fiber: 2g

Protein: 30g

Recipe 7: Air Fryer Lemon Pepper Chicken

Cooking time: 20 minutes

Prep time: 10 minutes

Servings: 4

Ingredients:

4 boneless, skinless chicken breasts

1 tsp. garlic powder

1 tsp. onion powder

1 tsp. black pepper

1 tsp. lemon pepper seasoning

2 tbsp. olive oil

1 lemon, sliced

Instructions:

Preheat the air fryer to 375°F.

In a small bowl, mix together the garlic powder, onion powder, black pepper, and lemon pepper seasoning.

Rub the chicken breasts with olive oil and then sprinkle the seasoning mixture over them.

Place the chicken breasts in the air fryer basket and add the lemon slices on top.

Cook for 18-20 minutes, or until the chicken is cooked through and reaches an internal temperature of 165°F.

Serve hot with your favorite side dish.

Nutrition per serving:

Calories: 233

Fat: 9g

Protein: 34g

Carbs: 2g

Fiber: 1g

Sugar: 0g

Sodium: 78mg

Recipe 8: Air Fryer Salmon with Broccoli

Cooking time: 12 minutes

Prep time: 10 minutes

Servings: 4

Ingredients:

4 salmon fillets, skin removed

2 cups broccoli florets

2 tbsp. olive oil

1 tsp. garlic powder

1 tsp. onion powder

1 tsp. paprika

Salt and pepper to taste

Instructions:

Preheat the air fryer to 400°F.

In a small bowl, mix together the garlic powder, onion powder, paprika, salt, and pepper.

Rub the salmon fillets with olive oil and then sprinkle the seasoning mixture over them.

Place the salmon fillets and broccoli florets in the air fryer basket.

Cook for 10-12 minutes, or until the salmon is cooked through and flakes easily with a fork.

Serve hot with a side of steamed rice.

Nutrition per serving:

Calories: 312

Fat: 18g

Protein: 32g

Carbs: 5g

Fiber: 2g

Sugar: 1g

Sodium: 97mg

Recipe 9: Air Fryer Chicken Thighs with Sweet Potato Fries

Cooking Time

25 minutes

Prep Time

15 minutes

Servings

4

Ingredients

4 chicken thighs

2 tbsp olive oil

Salt and pepper

2 sweet potatoes, cut into fries

1 tbsp cornstarch

1 tsp paprika

1 tsp garlic powder

1/2 tsp salt

Instructions

Preheat the air fryer to 400°F (200°C).

Brush the chicken thighs with olive oil and season with salt and pepper.

Place the chicken thighs in the air fryer basket and cook for 20-25 minutes or until the internal temperature reaches 165°F (74°C).

In a separate bowl, toss the sweet potato fries with cornstarch, paprika, garlic powder, and salt.

Add the sweet potato fries to the air fryer basket and cook for an additional 10-12 minutes, or until crispy and golden brown.

Serve the chicken thighs and sweet potato fries with your favorite dipping sauce.

Nutritional Information per Serving

Calories: 450

Fat: 24g

Carbohydrates: 28g

Fiber: 4g

Protein: 30g

Recipe 10: Air Fryer Shrimp and Vegetable Skewers
Cooking Time

15 minutes

Prep Time

20 minutes

Servings

4

Ingredients

16 large shrimp, peeled and deveined

1 red bell pepper, cut into chunks

1 yellow bell pepper, cut into chunks

1 zucchini, cut into chunks

1 tbsp olive oil

Salt and pepper

1 tsp garlic powder

Instructions

Preheat the air fryer to 400°F (200°C).

Thread the shrimp and vegetables onto skewers, alternating between shrimp and vegetables.

Brush the skewers with olive oil and season with salt, pepper, and garlic powder.

Place the skewers in the air fryer basket and cook for 10-12 minutes or until the shrimp are pink and cooked through.

Serve the shrimp and vegetable skewers with a side salad or brown rice.

Chapter 5: Desserts recipes

Recipe 1: Air Fryer Blueberry Crisp

Cooking time: 20 minutes

Prep time: 10 minutes

Servings: 4

Ingredients:

1 cup fresh blueberries

1/4 cup almond flour

1/4 cup rolled oats

1/4 cup chopped walnuts

1 tbsp honey

1 tbsp coconut oil

1 tsp ground cinnamon

Instructions:

Preheat the air fryer to 375°F.

In a mixing bowl, combine the almond flour, rolled oats, chopped walnuts, honey, coconut oil, and cinnamon. Mix well.

Add the blueberries to the mixture and stir gently.

Transfer the mixture to a baking dish that fits inside the air fryer basket.

Place the dish in the air fryer basket and cook for 20 minutes.

Serve warm.

Nutrition:

Calories: 170

Fat: 12g

Carbohydrates: 14g

Fiber: 3g

Protein: 4g

Recipe 2: Air Fryer Apple Chips

Cooking time: 15 minutes

Prep time: 5 minutes

Servings: 4

Ingredients:

2 medium-sized apples

1 tsp cinnamon

1 tsp coconut sugar

Instructions:

Preheat the air fryer to 375°F.

Wash the apples and slice them thinly, removing the cores.

In a mixing bowl, combine the cinnamon and coconut sugar.

Add the apple slices to the mixture and toss to coat.

Place the apple slices in the air fryer basket in a single layer.

Cook for 10-15 minutes, flipping the apple slices halfway through.

Serve immediately.

Nutrition:

Calories: 52

Fat: 0g

Carbohydrates: 14g

Fiber: 3g

Protein: 0g

Recipe 3: Air Fryer Chocolate Banana Bread

Cooking time: 35 minutes

Prep time: 15 minutes

Servings: 6

Ingredients:

2 ripe bananas

2 eggs

1/4 cup coconut flour

1/4 cup cocoa powder

1/4 cup honey

1 tsp baking powder

1 tsp vanilla extract

Pinch of salt

Cooking spray

Instructions:

Preheat the air fryer to 320°F.

In a mixing bowl, mash the bananas with a fork.

Add the eggs, coconut flour, cocoa powder, honey, baking powder, vanilla extract, and salt. Mix well.

Grease a small baking dish with cooking spray and pour the batter into the dish.

Place the dish in the air fryer basket and cook for 30-35 minutes.

Check the bread with a toothpick to ensure it's cooked through.

Let the bread cool for 10 minutes before slicing and serving.

Nutrition:

Calories: 125

Fat: 3g

Carbohydrates: 23g

Fiber: 4g

Protein: 4g

Recipe 4: Air Fryer Cinnamon Apple Chips

Cooking Time: 12 minutes

Prep Time: 10 minutes

Servings: 4

Ingredients:

2 medium-sized apples

1 tsp cinnamon

1 tsp sugar

Cooking spray

Instructions:

Preheat the air fryer to 375°F (190°C).

Cut the apples into thin slices, about 1/8-inch thick.

In a small bowl, mix together cinnamon and sugar.

Spray the air fryer basket with cooking spray.

Place the apple slices in a single layer in the air fryer basket.

Sprinkle the cinnamon and sugar mixture over the apple slices.

Air fry for 6 minutes, then flip the apple slices over.

Air fry for an additional 6 minutes, or until the apple chips are crisp and golden brown.

Serve and enjoy!

Nutrition per serving (4 servings total):

Calories: 48

Fat: 0.2g

Sodium: 0mg

Carbohydrates: 13g

Fiber: 2g

Sugar: 10g

Protein: 0.2g

Recipe 5: Air Fryer Banana Oatmeal Cookies

Cooking Time: 10 minutes

Prep Time: 15 minutes

Servings: 6

Ingredients:

2 ripe bananas, mashed

1 cup rolled oats

1/4 cup almond flour

1/4 cup unsweetened shredded coconut

1/4 cup raisins

1 tsp cinnamon

1/2 tsp vanilla extract

Cooking spray

Instructions:

Preheat the air fryer to 350°F (175°C).

In a medium-sized bowl, mash the bananas until smooth.

Add rolled oats, almond flour, shredded coconut, raisins, cinnamon, and vanilla extract to the bowl. Mix well.

Use a cookie scoop or tablespoon to form cookies, and place them on a parchment-lined air fryer basket.

Spray the cookies with cooking spray.

Air fry for 5 minutes.

Flip the cookies over and air fry for another 5 minutes.

Allow the cookies to cool on the air fryer basket for 5 minutes before serving.

Nutrition per serving (6 servings total):

Calories: 136

Fat: 5.5g

Sodium: 6mg

Carbohydrates: 21g

Fiber: 3g

Sugar: 8g

Protein: 3g

Recipe 6: Air Fryer Chocolate-Covered Strawberries

Cooking Time: 10 minutes

Prep Time: 15 minutes

Servings: 4

Ingredients:

8 large strawberries

1/4 cup dark chocolate chips

1 tsp coconut oil

Instructions:

Preheat the air fryer to 350°F (175°C).

Wash and dry the strawberries.

In a microwave-safe bowl, melt the dark chocolate chips and coconut oil together in the microwave for 30 seconds, then stir. Repeat until the chocolate is completely melted.

Dip the strawberries in the melted chocolate, and place them on a parchment-lined air fryer basket.

Air fry for 5 minutes.

Flip the strawberries over and air fry for another 5 minutes.

Allow the strawberries to cool on the air fryer basket for 5 minutes before serving.

Recipe 7: Air Fryer Berry Crumble

Prep time: 10 minutes

Cooking time: 15 minutes

Servings: 4

Ingredients:

2 cups mixed berries (fresh or frozen)

1/4 cup rolled oats

1/4 cup almond flour

1/4 cup chopped almonds

1 tbsp honey

1 tsp cinnamon

Instructions:

Preheat air fryer to 375°F (190°C).

In a mixing bowl, mix together the berries, honey, and cinnamon until well combined.

In another mixing bowl, mix together the rolled oats, almond flour, and chopped almonds.

Place the berry mixture into a small baking dish and sprinkle the oat mixture on top.

Place the baking dish in the air fryer basket and cook for 12-15 minutes or until the crumble is crispy and golden brown.

Serve warm.

Nutrition per serving:

Calories: 120

Total fat: 6 g

Saturated fat: 0.5 g

Cholesterol: 0 mg

Sodium: 2 mg

Total Carbohydrate: 16 g

Dietary fiber: 4 g

Sugar: 9 g

Protein: 3 g

Recipe 8: Air Fryer Baked Apples
Prep Time: 5 minutes

Cook Time: 15 minutes

Servings: 4

Ingredients:

4 medium-sized apples

2 tablespoons of honey

1 teaspoon of cinnamon

1 tablespoon of coconut oil

Instructions:

Preheat the air fryer to 350°F.

Cut the apples in half and remove the core.

In a small bowl, mix the honey and cinnamon together.

Brush the apples with coconut oil.

Place the apples in the air fryer basket and spoon the honey and cinnamon mixture on top of each apple.

Cook for 15 minutes.

Serve warm.

Nutrition:

Calories: 130

Fat: 2g

Carbohydrates: 30g

Protein: 0g

Fiber: 4g

Recipe 9: Air Fryer Chocolate Chip Cookies

Prep Time: 10 minutes

Cook Time: 8 minutes

Servings: 6

Ingredients:

1/2 cup unsalted butter, softened

1/2 cup granulated sugar

1/2 cup brown sugar

1 large egg

1 tsp vanilla extract

1 1/4 cups all-purpose flour

1/2 tsp baking soda

1/2 tsp salt

1 cup semisweet chocolate chips

Instructions:

Preheat your air fryer to 350°F.

In a mixing bowl, cream together the softened butter, granulated sugar, and brown sugar until light and fluffy.

Add the egg and vanilla extract and mix until well combined.

In a separate bowl, whisk together the flour, baking soda, and salt.

Add the flour mixture to the butter mixture and mix until just combined.

Fold in the chocolate chips.

Scoop tablespoonfuls of the dough onto a baking sheet and flatten them slightly.

Place the cookies in a single layer in the air fryer basket.

Air fry for 8 minutes or until the cookies are golden brown.

Let the cookies cool for a few minutes before serving.

Nutrition Information (per serving):

Calories: 453

Total Fat: 23 g

Saturated Fat: 14 g

Cholesterol: 66 mg

Sodium: 200 mg

Total Carbohydrate: 61 g

Dietary Fiber: 2 g

Sugar: 42 g

Protein: 4 g

Recipe 10: Air Fryer Banana Chips

Cooking time: 20 minutes

Prep time: 10 minutes

Servings: 4

Ingredients:

2 ripe bananas

1 tsp ground cinnamon

Cooking spray

Instructions:

Preheat your air fryer to 375°F.

Peel the bananas and slice them into thin rounds.

Lightly spray the banana slices with cooking spray and sprinkle with the ground cinnamon.

Place the banana slices in the air fryer basket in a single layer. Cook for 10 minutes.

After 10 minutes, flip the banana slices and cook for another 10 minutes until crispy and golden brown.

Serve as a healthy snack or dessert.

Nutrition per serving:

Calories: 58

Fat: 0.2g

Carbohydrates: 15g

Protein: 0.7g

Fiber: 2g

Sugar: 8g

Chapter 6: Snacks recipes

Recipe 1: Air Fryer Sweet Potato Fries

Cooking time: 15 minutes

Prep time: 10 minutes

Servings: 4

Ingredients:

2 large sweet potatoes, peeled and sliced into fries

1 tablespoon olive oil

1 teaspoon smoked paprika

1 teaspoon garlic powder

1/2 teaspoon salt

Fresh parsley, chopped (optional)

Instructions:

Preheat the air fryer to 400°F (200°C).

In a large bowl, toss the sweet potato fries with olive oil, smoked paprika, garlic powder, and salt until evenly coated.

Place the seasoned fries in the air fryer basket in a single layer, making sure not to overcrowd.

Cook for 15 minutes or until golden brown and crispy, flipping halfway through.

Serve hot, garnished with chopped parsley if desired.

Nutrition per serving:

Calories: 140

Fat: 3g

Carbohydrates: 27g

Protein: 2g

Fiber: 4g

Sugar: 6g

Sodium: 328mg

Recipe 2: Air Fryer Cauliflower Bites
Cooking time: 12 minutes

Prep time: 10 minutes

Servings: 4

Ingredients:

1 head cauliflower, cut into bite-sized florets

1/4 cup whole wheat flour

1/4 cup almond milk

1 teaspoon smoked paprika

1/2 teaspoon garlic powder

1/4 teaspoon salt

Cooking spray

Ranch dressing, for dipping (optional)

Instructions:

Preheat the air fryer to 375°F (190°C).

In a large bowl, whisk together the flour, almond milk, smoked paprika, garlic powder, and salt until a smooth batter forms.

Dip each cauliflower floret into the batter, making sure it's evenly coated, and then place it on a lightly greased air fryer basket.

Spray the florets with cooking spray and then place the basket in the air fryer.

Cook for 12 minutes or until crispy and golden brown, flipping the florets halfway through.

Serve hot with ranch dressing for dipping if desired.

Nutrition per serving:

Calories: 85

Fat: 2g

Carbohydrates: 15g

Protein: 4g

Fiber: 5g

Sugar: 3g

Sodium: 210mg

Recipe 3: Air Fryer Salmon Bites

Cooking time: 10 minutes

Prep time: 10 minutes

Servings: 4

Ingredients:

1 pound salmon fillet, skin removed and cut into bite-sized pieces

1/4 cup whole wheat flour

1 teaspoon garlic powder

1/2 teaspoon smoked paprika

1/4 teaspoon salt

Cooking spray

Lemon wedges, for serving

Instructions:

Preheat the air fryer to 400°F (200°C).

In a large bowl, whisk together the flour, garlic powder, smoked paprika, and salt until well combined.

Add the salmon pieces to the bowl and toss until evenly coated with the flour mixture.

Lightly spray the air fryer basket with cooking spray and place the salmon pieces in a single layer.

Recipe 4: Air Fryer Zucchini Chips

Cooking time: 15 minutes

Prep time: 10 minutes

Servings: 2

Ingredients:

2 medium zucchinis

1/2 cup whole wheat breadcrumbs

1/4 cup grated Parmesan cheese

1 tsp garlic powder

1/2 tsp salt

1 egg, beaten

Instructions:

Preheat your air fryer to 375°F.

Wash and slice the zucchinis into thin rounds.

In a bowl, mix together the breadcrumbs, Parmesan cheese, garlic powder, and salt.

Dip the zucchini slices into the beaten egg, then coat them with the breadcrumb mixture.

Place the coated zucchini slices in the air fryer basket and cook for 10-15 minutes, flipping them halfway through.

Once they are crispy and golden brown, remove the zucchini chips from the air fryer and serve them hot.

Nutrition (per serving):

Calories: 201

Total Fat: 6g

Saturated Fat: 2g

Cholesterol: 67mg

Sodium: 701mg

Total Carbohydrate: 25g

Dietary Fiber: 5g

Sugars: 6g

Protein: 12g

Recipe 5: Air Fryer Chicken Skewers

Cooking time: 15 minutes

Prep time: 10 minutes

Servings: 2

Ingredients:

2 boneless, skinless chicken breasts, cut into 1-inch cubes

1/4 cup low-sodium soy sauce

1/4 cup honey

1 tbsp sesame oil

1 tsp garlic powder

1/4 tsp black pepper

4 wooden skewers, soaked in water for 30 minutes

Instructions:

Preheat your air fryer to 400°F.

In a bowl, whisk together the soy sauce, honey, sesame oil, garlic powder, and black pepper.

Add the chicken cubes to the bowl and toss them until they are coated with the marinade.

Thread the chicken cubes onto the skewers.

Place the skewers in the air fryer basket and cook for 12-15 minutes, flipping them halfway through.

Chapter 6: Appetizers

Recipe 1: Air Fryer Chicken Wings

Prep Time: 10 minutes

Cook Time: 25 minutes

Servings: 4

Ingredients:

1 pound chicken wings, tips removed and drumettes and flats separated

1 tablespoon olive oil

1 teaspoon garlic powder

1 teaspoon paprika

1/2 teaspoon salt

1/4 teaspoon black pepper

1/4 cup hot sauce (optional)

Instructions:

Preheat the air fryer to 400°F (200°C).

In a large bowl, toss the chicken wings with olive oil, garlic powder, paprika, salt, and black pepper until evenly coated.

Arrange the chicken wings in a single layer in the air fryer basket.

Cook for 25 minutes, flipping the wings halfway through, until they are crispy and cooked through.

If desired, toss the wings in hot sauce before serving.

Nutrition (per serving):

Calories: 238

Total Fat: 17.7g

Saturated Fat: 4.2g

Cholesterol: 74mg

Sodium: 533mg

Total Carbohydrates: 1.3g

Dietary Fiber: 0.3g

Sugars: 0.3g

Protein: 17.9g

Recipe 2: Air Fryer Vegetable Spring Rolls

Prep time: 20 minutes

Cooking time: 10 minutes

Servings: 4

Ingredients:

8 spring roll wrappers

1 cup of thinly sliced cabbage

1 cup of thinly sliced carrots

1 cup of thinly sliced red bell peppers

1 cup of thinly sliced green onions

2 tablespoons of low-sodium soy sauce

1 tablespoon of rice vinegar

1 teaspoon of minced garlic

1 teaspoon of minced ginger

2 tablespoons of cornstarch

2 tablespoons of water

Cooking spray

Instructions:

In a bowl, mix together cabbage, carrots, bell peppers, green onions, soy sauce, rice vinegar, garlic, and ginger.

Lay a spring roll wrapper on a clean work surface and add 2 tablespoons of the vegetable mixture to the center of the wrapper.

Roll the wrapper tightly, tucking in the sides as you go, and use a bit of water to seal the edge.

In a small bowl, mix together cornstarch and water to form a paste.

Brush the spring rolls with the cornstarch mixture and spray lightly with cooking spray.

Preheat the air fryer to 375°F and cook the spring rolls for 10 minutes, flipping halfway through, until they are crispy and golden brown.

Serve hot with a low-sodium dipping sauce of your choice.

Nutrition:

Calories: 125

Fat: 1.6g

Carbohydrates: 23g

Protein: 4g

Sodium: 356mg

Recipe 3: Air Fryer Parmesan Zucchini Fries

Cooking Time: 10-12 minutes

Prep Time: 15 minutes

Servings: 4

Ingredients:

2 medium zucchinis

1/2 cup grated parmesan cheese

1/2 cup panko breadcrumbs

1 tablespoon Italian seasoning

1/2 teaspoon garlic powder

2 eggs, beaten

Salt and pepper to taste

Instructions:

Preheat the air fryer to 375°F.

Cut the zucchinis into thin, fry-like strips.

In a mixing bowl, combine parmesan cheese, panko breadcrumbs, Italian seasoning, garlic powder, salt, and pepper.

Dip the zucchini strips in the beaten eggs, then coat them with the breadcrumb mixture.

Place the coated zucchini strips in the air fryer basket in a single layer.

Cook for 10-12 minutes or until golden brown and crispy, flipping them halfway through the cooking time.

Serve immediately with dipping sauce of your choice.

Nutrition Information (per serving):

Calories: 155

Fat: 8g

Carbohydrates: 12g

Protein: 11g

Sodium: 475mg

Recipe 4: Air Fryer Garlic Parmesan Shrimp

Prep time: 10 minutes

Cook time: 8 minutes

Servings: 4

Ingredients:

1 pound large shrimp, peeled and deveined

2 cloves garlic, minced

1/4 cup grated Parmesan cheese

1/4 cup panko bread crumbs

1/4 teaspoon salt

1/4 teaspoon black pepper

2 tablespoons olive oil

Instructions:

Preheat air fryer to 400°F (200°C).

In a bowl, combine garlic, Parmesan cheese, bread crumbs, salt, and black pepper.

Add shrimp to the bowl and toss to coat.

Drizzle olive oil over the shrimp and toss again.

Place shrimp in a single layer in the air fryer basket.

Cook for 8 minutes, flipping halfway through.

Serve immediately.

Nutritional information per serving:

Calories: 218

Fat: 10g

Protein: 26g

Carbohydrates: 5g

Fiber: 0g

Sugar: 0g

Sodium: 521mg

Recipe 5: Turkey Meatballs

Prep time: 15 minutes

Cook time: 12 minutes

Servings: 4

Ingredients:

1 lb. ground turkey

1/2 cup almond flour

1 egg

2 cloves garlic, minced

1/2 tsp. salt

1/4 tsp. black pepper

1/4 cup chopped fresh parsley

Cooking spray

Instructions:

Preheat your air fryer to 375°F.

In a large bowl, combine ground turkey, almond flour, egg, garlic, salt, pepper, and parsley.

Mix everything together with your hands until well combined.

Shape mixture into 1 1/2-inch meatballs.

Spray the air fryer basket with cooking spray.

Arrange meatballs in a single layer in the air fryer basket.

Air fry for 12 minutes, flipping the meatballs halfway through.

Serve hot.

Nutrition per serving (4 servings):

Calories: 227

Fat: 13g

Carbohydrates: 5g

Protein: 24g

Chapter 7: 28-Days Air Fryer Meal Plan to Detox and Cleanse the liver

Day 1:

Breakfast: Air-fried egg and vegetable omelet

Lunch: Air-fried salmon with roasted asparagus

Dinner: Air-fried chicken breast with sweet potato fries

Day 2:

Breakfast: Air-fried breakfast sausage with scrambled eggs

Lunch: Air-fried shrimp with a side salad

Dinner: Air-fried pork chops with roasted Brussels sprouts

Day 3:

Breakfast: Air-fried avocado and egg toast

Lunch: Air-fried tofu with mixed vegetables

Dinner: Air-fried steak with roasted cauliflower

Day 4:

Breakfast: Air-fried bacon and eggs

Lunch: Air-fried chicken wings with celery sticks and ranch dressing

Dinner: Air-fried tilapia with roasted green beans

Day 5:

Breakfast: Air-fried breakfast burrito with scrambled eggs, black beans, and avocado

Lunch: Air-fried turkey breast with a side salad

Dinner: Air-fried pork tenderloin with roasted carrots

Day 6:

Breakfast: Air-fried cinnamon apples with Greek yogurt

Lunch: Air-fried chicken drumsticks with a side of roasted squash

Dinner: Air-fried salmon patties with roasted broccoli

Day 7:

Breakfast: Air-fried breakfast sausage and vegetable hash

Lunch: Air-fried shrimp and vegetable skewers with a side of quinoa

Dinner: Air-fried turkey burger with roasted sweet potato wedges

Day 8:

Breakfast: Scrambled eggs with avocado and cherry tomatoes

Lunch: Grilled chicken salad with mixed greens, cucumbers, and cherry tomatoes

Dinner: Air-fried salmon with roasted asparagus and quinoa

Day 9:

Breakfast: Greek yogurt with fresh berries and almonds

Lunch: Air-fried turkey burger with sweet potato fries

Dinner: Air-fried tofu with mixed vegetables and brown rice

Day 10:

Breakfast: Oatmeal with sliced banana and honey

Lunch: Air-fried chicken tenders with carrot and celery sticks

Dinner: Air-fried shrimp with zucchini noodles and garlic sauce

Day 11:

Breakfast: Spinach and feta omelet with whole-grain toast

Lunch: Air-fried turkey meatballs with marinara sauce and roasted broccoli

Dinner: Air-fried pork chops with roasted sweet potatoes and Brussels sprouts

Day 12:

Breakfast: Avocado toast with sliced tomato and a poached egg

Lunch: Air-fried fish tacos with cabbage slaw and salsa

Dinner: Air-fried chicken thighs with roasted carrots and mashed sweet potatoes

Day 13:

Breakfast: Greek yogurt with granola and sliced fruit

Lunch: Air-fried vegetable spring rolls with peanut sauce

Dinner: Air-fried beef and vegetable stir-fry with brown rice

Day 14:

Breakfast: Smoothie bowl with frozen berries, banana, almond milk, and chia seeds

Lunch: Air-fried chicken drumsticks with cucumber salad

Dinner: Air-fried cod with roasted asparagus and quinoa

Day 15

Breakfast:

Scrambled eggs with diced vegetables (bell pepper, onion, and mushroom)

1 slice of whole grain toast

Fresh berries

Lunch:

Grilled chicken breast

Air-fried sweet potato fries

Side salad with mixed greens and tomatoes

Dinner:

Air-fried salmon

Roasted asparagus spears

Quinoa pilaf

Day 16

Breakfast:

Greek yogurt with honey and mixed berries

1 slice of whole grain toast

Lunch:

Air-fried chicken drumsticks

Roasted Brussels sprouts

Brown rice

Dinner:

Air-fried tofu with stir-fried vegetables (carrots, zucchini, bell peppers, and broccoli)

Whole wheat noodles

Day 17

Breakfast:

Overnight oats with chia seeds and sliced almonds

1 banana

Lunch:

Air-fried turkey burgers

Sweet potato wedges

Side salad with mixed greens and tomatoes

Dinner:

Air-fried shrimp

Roasted root vegetables (carrots, turnips, and beets)

Brown rice

Day 18

Breakfast:

Avocado toast with a fried egg

Fresh fruit salad

Lunch:

Air-fried chicken wings

Roasted cauliflower

Quinoa salad with mixed vegetables

Dinner:

Air-fried pork chops

Roasted green beans

Mashed sweet potatoes

Day 19

Breakfast:

Greek yogurt with honey and mixed berries

1 slice of whole grain toast

Lunch:

Air-fried chicken tenders

Roasted sweet potato wedges

Side salad with mixed greens and tomatoes

Dinner:

Air-fried cod

Grilled asparagus spears

Brown rice

Day 20

Breakfast:

Scrambled eggs with diced vegetables (bell pepper, onion, and mushroom)

1 slice of whole grain toast

Fresh berries

Lunch:

Air-fried chicken thighs

Roasted Brussels sprouts

Brown rice

Dinner:

Air-fried turkey breast

Roasted root vegetables (carrots, turnips, and beets)

Quinoa pilaf

Day 21

Breakfast:

Overnight oats with chia seeds and sliced almonds

1 banana

Lunch:

Air-fried fish sticks

Roasted green beans

Quinoa salad with mixed vegetables

Dinner:

Air-fried shrimp

Grilled asparagus spears

Brown rice

Day 22:

Breakfast: Greek yogurt with sliced almonds and blueberries

Lunch: Air-fried salmon with a side of roasted asparagus

Dinner: Air-fried chicken breast with a side of roasted sweet potato wedges

Day 23:

Breakfast: Avocado and egg toast

Lunch: Air-fried turkey burger with lettuce and tomato on a whole wheat bun

Dinner: Air-fried cod with a side of roasted Brussels sprouts

Day 24:

Breakfast: Omelet with spinach, tomato, and feta cheese

Lunch: Air-fried chicken and vegetable skewers with quinoa

Dinner: Air-fried pork chops with a side of roasted butternut squash

Day 25:

Breakfast: Overnight oats with sliced banana and honey

Lunch: Air-fried shrimp with a side of roasted broccoli

Dinner: Air-fried tofu with a side of roasted carrots

Day 26:

Breakfast: Smoothie bowl with Greek yogurt, berries, and granola

Lunch: Air-fried chicken Caesar salad

Dinner: Air-fried salmon with a side of roasted cauliflower

Day 27:

Breakfast: Scrambled eggs with whole wheat toast and sliced avocado

Lunch: Air-fried turkey meatballs with a side of roasted zucchini

Dinner: Air-fried chicken thighs with a side of roasted green beans

Day 28:

Breakfast: Greek yogurt with sliced peaches and walnuts

Lunch: Air-fried shrimp tacos with avocado salsa and whole wheat tortillas

Dinner: Air-fried cod with a side of roasted asparagus

Thank you for reading

For enquiry, contact the author through gmail;

Adamubwada@gmail.com

Printed in Great Britain
by Amazon

27133202R00066